LES TEMPS
DE
NOS JOURS

ALVAR

Introduction

Let us imagine one day as a symbol
and as a summary of all the many days
that we experience during a lifetime.

This is the theme that the artist expresses
in the four lithographs comprising
"The Times Of Our Days."

From the freshness of dawn…
to the blaze of noon…
to the mellowness of afternoon…
to the intimacy of evening…
we follow the cycle of the sun
and the course of a family's life.

Circles of time
like the hands that sweep a clock…
Cycles of life
like the rings that grow within the trunk of a tree…

"Matin" (Morning – Childhood)

5/190

A *new day* … The sun is rising … its soft rays illuminate the tender colors of nature's palette at springtime … its arousing warmth persuades flowers to open and plants to grow.

Three children, as fresh as the morning, commence their day. One skips rope, another flies a kite, the third plays a classic flute … childhood play … the start of activities.

The gentle waves of the sea stretch across the horizon as the tide comes in.

Symbolically, a young tree begins to sprout its first leaves …

"Midi" (Noontime – Youth)

The sun climbs
to the top of the sky…
a dazzling source
of light, color and
energy.

With youthful delight
two figures link arms
as they look into
each other's eyes
and into the future
they wish to build
together.

A pair of doves,
the artist's symbol
of hope and grace,
appears to alight on
their outstretched hands.

In brightly colored
and flowing robes
the couple dances
through fields that
thrive with life
at the onset of summer.

The sea at high tide
rolls giant spirals
of waves along the
coast – where
two leafy trees,
their roots intertwined,
have blossomed…

7/190

"Après-Midi" (Afternoon – Adulthood)

The afternoon sun
glows warmly
above the horizon…

The artist equates
this third part of the
day with early autumn
and the harvest.

Embossed at lower right,
a table still-life
includes a bowl of
ripened fruit and a
pitcher of wine
from grapes like those
atop the rustic stool.

Three trees,
laden with apples,
bask in the sunlight…
in the azure serenity
of an ebbing sea.

A child runs along
the tiled floor to the
interior of the house
and the welcoming embrace
of the father.

The child reaches for
the geometric objects
that appear at upper right,
the artist's symbols
of our quest for
knowledge and communication.

This puzzle of geometries,
not yet within the
child's grasp,
will be reached…
with time…
and with maturity.

"Soir" (Evening – Maturity)

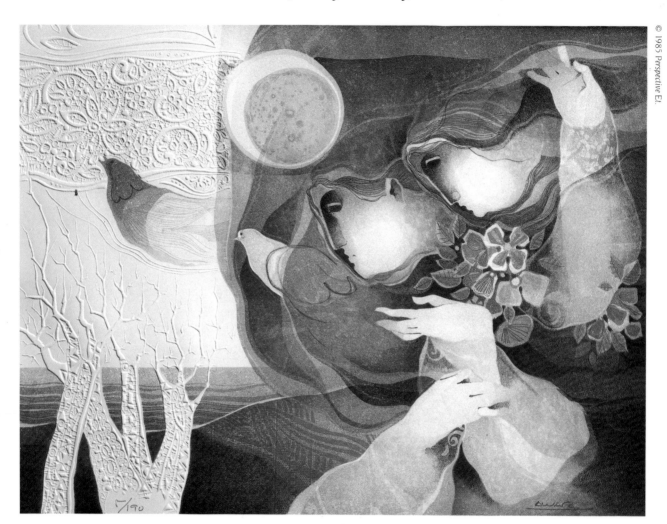

Beyond the horizon the sun continues its cycle. The blue shades of evening usher in a crescent moon. The sea is calm at ebb tide. Four trees keep vigil along the coast.

Tranquility … maturity … contemplation of the patterns of creation and continuation … the enjoyment of more cycles to come …

Their child having grown up, the couple is together again … appreciating the rewards of life … the fruit of the seed that was planted, that blossomed, and was nurtured.

Two doves fly into the lace-like space of the sky … a flight of time … A time to dream and to rediscover each other …

Alvar was born in the Catalan coastal village of Montgat near Barcelona in 1935. He started painting in oils at age twelve, and at age seventeen was accepted at the Escuela Superior de Bellas Artes in Barcelona. During this period one of his paintings was acquired by the Museum of Modern Art in Barcelona for its permanent collection. Before graduating from the Bellas Artes he was given his first one-man show, Barcelona, 1957. In the following year the Institut Français awarded him a scholarship to study in Paris, where he eventually settled for a number of years.

Since a decisive one-man show in Paris, 1963, he has exhibited regularly throughout Europe, the United States, Canada and Japan.

In 1978 a retrospective exhibition of his lithographs was held by the Musée Hyacinthe Rigaud in Perpignan, France. His lithographs, paintings and sculpture have been presented in major shows at the Utah Museum of Fine Arts, Salt Lake City, 1982, and at the Wichita Art Museum, 1983. The Kumamoto Museum and the Fukuoka Museum, both in Kyushu, Japan, have purchased his lithographs for their permanent collections.

Since 1963 Alvar has devoted much of his time and talent to the creation of original lithographs. Starting from a simple drawing idea, he creates directly on the plates with spontaneity, deciding during the process how many colors to use (between seven and twelve), where to augment or diminish in order to achieve maximum effect from the superimposition of the colors when printing the plates. A close look at his graphic work will reveal a wealth of textures, color gradations, draughtsmanship and innovative techniques.